Preparing for Adolescence

Advice from One of America's
Foremost Family Psychologists
on How to Survive the
Coming Years
of Change

Growth Guide

A workbook to be used with the million copy
best-selling book *Preparing for Adolescence.*

DR. JAMES DOBSON

Preparing for Adolescence

Advice from One of America's Foremost Family Psychologists on How to Survive the Coming Years of Change

Growth Guide

A workbook to be used with the million copy best-selling book *Preparing for Adolescence*.

Regal

A Division of Gospel Light
Ventura, California, U.S.A.

Published by Regal Books
A Division of Gospel Light
Ventura, California 93006
Printed in U.S.A.

Regal Books is a ministry of Gospel Light, an evangelical Christian publisher dedicated to serving the local church. We believe God's vision for Gospel Light is to provide church leaders with biblical, user-friendly materials that will help them evangelize, disciple and minister to children, youth and families.

It is our prayer that this Regal Book will help you discover biblical truth for your own life and help you meet the needs of others. May God richly bless you.

For a free catalog of resources from Regal Books/Gospel Light please contact your Christian supplier or call 1-800-4-GOSPEL.

PREPARING FOR ADOLESCENCE GROWTH GUIDE
© Copyright 1979 by Vision House
All rights reserved.

Library of Congress Catalog Number 78-57673

9 10 11 12 13 14 15 / 01 00 99 98

Rights for publishing this book in other languages are contracted by Gospel Literature International (GLINT). GLINT also provides technical help for the adaptation, translation and publishing of Bible study resources and books in scores of languages worldwide. For further information, contact GLINT, P.O. Box 4060, Ontario, CA 91761-1003, U.S.A., or the publisher.

This book
is affectionately dedicated
to my teenager
and all the other young people
whom I have come to love
as my own.

Contents

Introduction

This workbook is designed to reinforce the understandings included in my book, *Preparing for Adolescence* (and the cassette tape album by the same name). It can be used by teachers who are leading class discussions, or it can be of assistance to parents who want to teach their own "children." Finally, preteens and teenagers may want to answer the workbook questions on their own, in an attempt to get acquainted with themselves. The material is written to accommodate all three approaches.

Let's begin, now, with the first lesson which introduces the subject of adolescence (and its most painful experience: feelings of inferiority). I hope you find this workbook helpful and encouraging. If you do, then we both owe a word of appreciation to Ted Zebel for his inspiration and assistance to this project and to Carol Bostrom, who did most of the original writing.

God bless you,

James C. Dobson, Ph.D.

Caution! Bridge Out Ahead!

Before you explore this chapter of the *Growthguide*, read pages 13-27 of **Chapter 1 of** *Preparing for Adolescence*, by Dr. James Dobson.

What is "adolescence" (pronunciation: ad'l ESS ens), according to the **first paragraph of** Chapter 1?

3

Here's another definition: "The state or process of growing up from childhood to adulthood." The word comes from the Latin word *adolescere*, which means "to grow up." So "adolescence" is just a big word for "growing up."

How old are you? Circle your age below.

9   10   11   12 | 13   14   15   16   17   18   19

looking forward →   involved in adolescence

Growing up isn't easy. Life is always making new demands on you. When your life first started, you were safe and warm inside your mother's body, protected from harm, hearing her heart beating steadily.

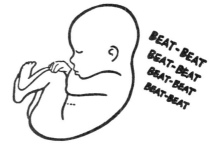

BEAT-BEAT
BEAT-BEAT
BEAT-BEAT
BEAT-BEAT

But you couldn't stay there. You were forced out into the cold world, where a doctor held you up by your heels and whacked your bottom till you cried. (He did this for your own good—to get your lungs working—but *you* didn't know that!)

Here's a cartoon showing a newborn baby being spanked by a doctor. Make up a caption to show what the baby would say, if he could speak, about what has just happened to him and how he feels about it.

Moving into adolescence can be just as painful and scary as being born. But the *Preparing for Adolescence* book and Growthguide, along with the assistance of your parents or other adults, can help you avoid some of the worst problems and do a better job of dealing with others.

In Chapter 1 of *Preparing for Adolescence* there's a story about *you* driving down a road. Here's a picture of your car driving along. It represents your life. Put on it a symbol representing you, or make up a C.B. "handle" for yourself and write it on the car.

As you're driving along, you meet a flagman.

4

What does the flagman tell you about the road ahead? (See page 16 in *Preparing for Adolescence* and fill in a summary in the flagman's "balloon.")

What solution to the problem does the flagman suggest?
SOLUTION:

What is the "canyon" that most teenagers fall into? (Write the name at the bottom of the canyon below.)

Here are statements by some people who have fallen into the "canyon."

In the blanks, put comments you have heard others say, or problems you have felt yourself.

Do you ever feel like hiding in a hole or cave?

Do you ever wish you had someone
else's body instead of your own?

These are signs you are feeling . . .

Most teenagers decide they are without much human worth when they are 13 to 15 years old.

What does God say about the worth of a human being? Read the following verses and see what they say about human worth.

Genesis 1:27-31 _____

_____

Psalm 8 _____

_____

Philippians 2:5-11 _____

_____

John 3:16 _____

_____

WHY do American young people feel inferior? There are three characteristics that teens think they must have in order to feel good about themselves. If they don't have these features, they feel inferior. The three things are . . .

NO.1-PHYSICAL ATTRACTIVENESS

FACT: about 80 percent of the teenagers in our society don't like the way they look. Let's just repeat that figure here:

_____ *percent*

What are some things you don't like about the way *you* look?

Often friends say unkind things about the way you look, or call you nicknames that hurt. What nickname has upset you?

Do you know someone at school who feels terribly inferior because of his or her looks? Describe that person and explain how you know he or she is unhappy.

Has there ever been a time when you were not invited to an important event, or when you were not chosen for something you really cared about? Describe your feelings at those times.

Have you ever felt self-conscious at the beach, at the swimming pool, or in the showers after gym class? What part of your body embarrasses you in such a situation?

Is there another person whose looks you admire and envy? Describe how this person looks and why you feel envious.

Many young people feel they aren't very smart—that they are plain *dumb*. And this causes a lot of inferiority feelings. What do you think—are you smart, or dumb, or in-between?

NO. 2 - INTELLIGENCE

Describe a time in your childhood when you felt that others thought you were unintelligent.

Have you ever had a serious problem with your schoolwork? Describe your problem and the feelings you had about it.

Is there something you would like to be able to do, but you're afraid you aren't intelligent enough to learn how to do it?

Does your school have special groups or classes to which students are assigned on the basis of their ability (such as low and high reading or math groups, or a gifted students' class)? How do you feel about the highest group? The lowest group? The one you are in?

NO. 3 - MONEY

Many teens feel that their families have to have enough money for the "right" kind of home, car, clothing, and so on. If they don't have material things like those their friends have, they feel inferior.

Is lack of money a problem to you?

For the next lesson, read the rest of Chapter 1 of *Preparing for Adolescence*. In this part of the chapter you will find suggestions for getting out of the canyon of inferiority.

Parent/Teacher Instructions

Have your child follow along in and use the Growthguide as you go through the lesson.

Definition of adolescence: for a class, have the definitions from *Preparing for Adolescence* and from the Growthguide prepared in advance on posterboard, chalkboard, or overhead projector transparency. Display the definitions so everyone can see them, and then go over them briefly.

Have the student circle his or her age on the chart in the Growthguide.

Briefly go through the "Growing-Up-Isn't-Easy" material.

"New baby" cartoon: parent and child discuss and decide on a caption. Let the child fill it in. In a class setting, have each student do his or her caption individually; then have a few students share.

Car and flagman: have a young person create a symbol or C.B. "handle" to represent himself or herself, and write or draw the symbol on the car picture. If the student has read the chapter in *Preparing for Adolescence*, ask him to tell you the flagman's warning and suggested solution. If he has not read the chapter, provide this information for him. Allow time for him to write summaries in his Growthguide. Consider acting out the conversation between the driver and the flagman, with yourself taking the flagman role.

If the student has read the chapter in *Preparing for Adolescence*, ask him to give the name of the canyon. If he hasn't read it, direct him to pages 16 and 17 of the book, and have him read the section under the heading "The Agony of Inferiority." Have him fill in the name at the bottom of the canyon drawing.

Go through the comments made by teens who feel inferior; then discuss what the student has heard from others or felt himself. Let him fill in the two blank captions.

Parent and child should discuss whether the child has ever felt like "hiding in a hole" or "crawling into another's body." In a class, simply let students think about these for a moment. Ask, "Whose body would you prefer? In other words, who do you admire, and why?" Ask, "Is that other person actually more valuable as a human being than you? How does *God* compare the two of you?"

Give the statement from the Growthguide that most teenagers decide they are without much human worth when they are between 13 and 15 years of age. Work with your child to read the Scriptures and determine what they say about human worth. There are suggestions below to help you with this. (In a classroom, divide students into four groups to read the Scriptures, work out their application to human value, and then report to the class.)

Genesis 1:27-31: the creation account. God *created* us, and anything He makes has value. In addition, He made us *in His image*, which adds infinitely to our worth. And He pronounced His handiwork (including humans) *good*. It is true that Adam and Eve sinned, and therefore we are all fallen and flawed. But we still have great value in God's eyes.

Psalm 8: the writer starts out feeling small and unworthy, but he sees how much God values mankind. God gives us the rule over the creation that He made on this earth. God crowns us with glory and majesty. God says we are only a little lower than His angels! (Some translations give "God" instead of "angels" here.)

Philippians 2:5-11: God thought we were of such great value that He sent His only Son to become one of us. Jesus was a real human being at the same time that He was really God and worthy of all glory and worship. The fact that God the Son made Himself like us gives us great worth.

John 3:16: this familiar verse reminds us of two things. First, God loves us. And that gives us value. Second, He thought enough of us to send His Son to die for us so that we might be saved from our sinful condition. So in God's eyes, we are of great worth.

Yet most young people don't realize how valuable they are in God's sight. They seek for value in *things*. I have found three main areas in which young people seek value. First, in physical attractiveness. Note the cartoon at the top of this section in the Growthguide. Many teens judge others and themselves on the basis of good looks.

Make sure your students understand what 80 percent means: 8 out of every 10, or 80 out of every 100. Have them fill in 80 percent in the blank to reinforce the figure.

Parent: discuss with your child the things he or she doesn't like about his or her appearance. *Teacher:* Have your students get together with one or two trusted friends to discuss their dislikes.

Follow the same format with the remaining questions in this section.

Review with your child or students the material on intelligence. This begins on page 26 of *Preparing for Adolescence,* under the heading "Who's Dumb?" If your child has already read this, have him or her tell you what it says.

Parent: discuss with your child the answers to the questions about intelligence. *Teacher:* let the students discuss in small groups as before.

Follow the same format for the section on money, using the information found on page 27 of *Preparing for Adolescence.*

Parent: when your child shares problems with you, *listen* carefully. Don't try to give the solutions now (unless there's a really obvious and simple one); and don't give glib reassurances like "It isn't really so bad," "It will work out," or "You'll outgrow it." These may all be true from *your* perspective, but problems seem much larger and more immediate to a young person than they do to an adult, and reassurances of this nature do little to help. Also avoid the temptation to tell your child how much better off he or she is than you were at the same age. The old line, "I walked three miles to school every day" only erects barriers.

Conversely, if you will share your *inner* life and tell your feelings, your child will be encouraged to do the same. I often find it helpful to give the painful details of a rejection or humiliation I felt in junior high school. This way I become a real human being to the young people with whom I'm working. They can identify with me. This type of sharing creates closeness rather than barriers.

Teacher: the classroom setting and time pressures may not allow you to discuss with each child his or her worries in the areas brought up in this session. But make yourself available after class for those who may need to talk to you *now.* Listen more than you talk, and be willing to share of yourself, as suggested in the comments above.

Close the lesson with prayer, committing problems to God and thanking Him for giving human beings great worth and value.

11

Lesson Two

This Way Out of the Canyon of Inferiority

Before beginning this study, read pages 29-32 of *Preparing for Adolescence.*

In our last session we talked about *problems*—the "canyon of inferiority" and the difficulties that cause young people to feel inferior.

This time (and also in Lesson 3) we're going to talk about *solutions.* If you have already fallen into the "canyon," these ideas will help you get out. If you have not yet fallen in, they can help you drive *around* the canyon.

SUGGESTION ONE: Remember That You Are Not Alone

You may not realize it, but other people have the same problems you do—feeling inferior for various reasons. But they may act in such a way that you don't realize they feel inferior. (And that's exactly what they are trying to achieve—hiding their bad feelings about themselves.)

Can you think of times when you have seen someone who is . . .

Shy and quiet

Angry and mean

Silly

Afraid to participate in a game or contest

Blushing frequently

Acting proud and "stuck up"

If you have, you have probably seen someone who is feeling *inferior.*

Have you ever acted in any of the ways on that list? How were *you* feeling at that time?

SUGGESTION TWO: Face Your Problems

It always seems to work better to face problems rather than try to ignore them. So . . .

List some things that bug you about yourself. I've given you a few examples below, and you can check off the ones that are true for you, and then add others.

_____ I get frustrated and angry too often

_____ I'm too shy

_____ I can't seem to say what I mean, to put my thoughts into words

_____ I'm lazy

_____ I do unkind things

_____ I don't like the way I look

_____ I'm not very smart

_____ _____

_____ _____

_____ _____

Go back and circle those examples that worry you the most.

Find a trusted older person (such as a parent or teacher) and talk to him or her about the items you have circled. With the help of that advisor, start to plan a strategy to solve the problems that can be solved. Here's a chart to use for one problem, just to give you an idea.

My problem is: _____

I've decided on the following long-range goal for dealing with this problem:

by _____
  (date)

I would like the following to be true:

_____

_____

_____

Here are some short-range steps I will take to reach that goal:

_____

_____

_____

You're on your way to solving some of your problems!

But there are others that you can't solve. What about them?

> *The best way to have a healthy mind*
> *is to learn to accept*
> *those things which you cannot change.*

If you can't solve it, you can learn to live with it. Better yet, you can commit it to God. As suggested in the book (page 32), plan to make a small, *safe* fire to burn a paper listing your unsolvable problems. Read the prayer on page 32 and then pray in your own words as you burn the paper. As a reminder, copy your prayer here:

God knows and cares about you and all of your problems. As I explained on page 33, He will honor your decision to depend on Him. Listed below are two Scripture passages that back up that statement. Read them, and then paraphrase them in such a way that they apply to the things you worry about. I've given an example using a different Scripture passage.

EXAMPLE:

Philippians 4:6, 7   *Paraphrase:*   *"I don't need to worry about any of these problems, because God invites me to pray about them instead, and to give Him thanks; and He will give me a peace that will help keep me from worrying about what cannot be changed."*

NOW YOU TRY:

Proverbs 3:5, 6   *Paraphrase:*   _____
                                       _____
                                       _____

1 Peter 5:6, 7   *Paraphrase:*   _____
                                       _____
                                       _____

Next time we'll talk about more ways out of the "canyon."

Parent/Teacher Instructions

Introduce the session by using ideas from the first part of the Growthguide lesson.

Briefly go through the section that begins, "Can you think of times . . . ." *Parent:* ask your child to describe occasions when he has seen people displaying the various behaviors. *Teacher:* take just a minute or two to get a few sample responses. *Both:* be sure to stress that the traits described indicate that the person is feeling inferior (even if the behavior seems to suggest "superior" feelings).

Parent: ask for your child's response to the question, "Have you ever acted in any of the ways on that list? How were you feeling at that time?" Don't make value judgments about behaviors and feelings. And be ready to share one or two of your experiences of feeling inferior.

Teacher: in a small class, ask for volunteers to give brief answers to the question discussed above. In a larger class, have students pair off and exchange experiences.

Let students mark the section, listing characteristics they don't like about themselves. *Parent:* take plenty of time to talk over these problems with your child. Again, don't make value judgments or minimize the seriousness of a young person's concerns. Use the chart to help your child make some plans for dealing with his or her most pressing problems.

Teacher: ask your students to name some of their problems in just a word or two. Jot them down and select one that seems to be most common. Apply the planning chart to that problem, getting the class to participate, so that they will see how to make specific plans to improve a difficult area. Encourage them to do the same for problems that have not been discussed.

Section on problems that cannot be solved: if you can, share a personal experience of such a problem and how you learned to commit it to God.

If possible, provide a metal wastebasket, fireplace, or other safe area for the "fire of commitment." Also provide blank paper which students can use to make their lists for burning.

Direct students in the Scripture paraphrase activity. *Parent and teacher:* make your own paraphrase ahead of time. Let it deal with a problem or problems you have, then share it with your students as an example.

Close the session with a prayer, thanking God that He is worthy of our trust and that He cares about our problems.

More Ways Out of the Canyon of Inferiority

This lesson is based on pages 33-39 of *Preparing for Adolescence.*

REVIEW

In the last lesson we looked at two suggestions for getting out of the canyon of inferiority: 1) remember that you are not alone, and 2) face your problem. In this chapter we will continue with more ideas for feeling better about yourself.

Sometimes young people (and adults, too) feel so inferior that they think God can't be interested in them or care about them, and that He certainly could never use them. If you've been thinking that way, you are in for a surprise. We're going to take a look at some of the people Jesus chose for His followers and friends. Their names are given on the chart on the following page, along with some Scriptures telling about them. Read the Scriptures and then fill in whatever they tell you about the occupation and characteristics of the men (what they were like as people).

JESUS' FOLLOWERS	OCCUPATION	CHARACTERISTICS
James and John Matthew 4:21, 22 Mark 3:16, 17; 10:35-41 Luke 9:51-56		
Matthew Matthew 9:9; 10:2, 3		
Peter Matthew 4:18; 16:21-23 Mark 9:1-6; 14:27-38, 54, 66-72		

18 *Moses*

Moses is another surprise. We hear about his mighty exploits for God. But sometimes we don't hear about his inferiority feelings. His life is summarized on pages 34 and 35 of *Preparing for Adolescence.*

When God wanted to give Moses a job to do, Moses made objections and God made promises. Read Exodus 4:1-14 and complete this chart of Moses' objections and God's promises.

MOSES' OBJECTIONS	GOD'S PROMISES

According to Exodus 4:14, how did God feel about Moses' continued objections?

REMEMBER: God doesn't want His people to get so worried about their "inferiority" that they can't trust the Almighty to do what He says He will do!

SORRY, GOD, I'M TOO INFERIOR. YOU WON'T BE ABLE TO WORK THROUGH ME!

Have you found any similarities between yourself and the men you have just studied? Write down ways that you are like each of these (if you are):

James

John

Peter

Matthew

Moses

If God could use them and love them, do you think He can use you and love you?

SUGGESTION THREE: Compensate

Compensation means making up for your weaknesses by developing your strengths . . . doing something that makes you feel proud of yourself. What are some skills you have, or activities you do well or really like to do?

Think about what you have listed. Can you pick one or two things and work hard to develop that special strong point, such as having a good personality? Circle those things you choose, and then jot down one or two ideas for getting started.

Talk your ideas over with a friend or trusted adult and get their suggestions too.

SUGGESTION FOUR: Have Genuine Friends

True friends will help your self-concept (the way you think about yourself). Do you have some good friends now? Think about one special friend and describe how he or she makes you feel good about yourself.

How are you at *being* a friend? Take a look at what the Bible says: read Proverbs 18:24 and Ephesians 4:32. Use the ideas from these two Scriptures to describe the kind of friend you would like to be.

FRIENDSHIP SCALE

Here are some suggestions from *Preparing for Adolescence* on being a friend. After each statement, give yourself a score, choosing a number from 1 to 5, with 1 meaning you are poor at the quality described, and 5 meaning you're very good at it.

Trait   *Score*

I respect people.

_____

I accept people.

_____

I let people know they are important to me.

_____

I am sensitive to others' feelings.

_____

I am kind.

_____

I am careful about what I say about others.

_____

I stay away from sarcasm.

_____

I am tolerant of others' mistakes.

_____

I stand up for my friends.

_____

I am understanding about other people's problems.

_____

I am a friend to the friendless.

_____

What's your total? _____

55-65: you're a super friend.
30-55: not bad, but could be better.
13-30: you need to work on it!

The point of this exercise is not to give yourself a "grade" and stop there. Rather, I hope this will start you thinking about how to be a good friend. Then having friends will come naturally.

FINAL SUGGESTION: Remember God's Values

Read Luke 16:15. Why does God despise what people treasure? (Review page 38 of *Preparing for Adolescence* if you need some ideas.)

In Lesson 1 we talked about three qualities most young people feel they must have in order to feel worthwhile: good looks, intelligence, and money. How do you suppose God feels about our values when we put these things above our relationships with people or with Him?

If you haven't yet suffered from feelings of inferiority, I hope you will remember to drive *around* the canyon instead of falling into it. Here's a reminder that will help: you will sometimes "hear" two voices inside you, something like this:

The encouraging voice will lead you around the canyon of inferiority; the negative voice will cause you to crash right to the canyon floor, if you let it. The choice is yours: *you* decide which voice to listen to, which voice to believe. I hope you'll listen to God's encouragement and drive safely around the danger!

Before the next lesson, read pages 41-50 in *Preparing for Adolescence.*

Parent/Teacher Instructions

Review the previous lesson. Ask your students if they have made any of the changes they discussed.

Introduce the Scripture study about people whom God chooses. If you can, relate a personal experience which you have had in not feeling God cared about you or would use you, and how you learned you were mistaken. *Parent:* work with your child to read and discuss the assigned Scriptures and to complete the chart about Jesus' followers. *Teacher:* let your students work in groups of two to four to complete the Scripture study; lead a brief general discussion of their findings, and use the ideas below to supplement as needed, particularly pointing out how God used these men.

James and John were fishermen—not rich, not well-educated, not scholars or theologians. They were nicknamed "Sons of Thunder," so they must have been temperamental, loud, and impulsive men. They missed the point of Jesus' message, and went so far as to ask for special privileges in His kingdom. They even wanted to command fire from heaven to destroy some people who did not receive Christ. Jesus knew the kind of men they were when He chose them—and He knew He could do something with them! James became a faithful disciple who was martyred in about 44 A.D. (see Acts 12:2). Jesus gave John the special mission of taking care of Mary, His mother. John wrote the Gospel of John, three New Testament letters, and the Book of Revelation. He was bold of speech and action for the spread of the gospel: Jesus made something beautiful out of the "thunder" of his personality. For years John was one of the main leaders of the church in Jerusalem. In his writings he stressed the theme of love.

Matthew was a tax-collector. We don't know much about his personality, but we know from history that tax-collectors were hated because they used their office to extort extra money out of the taxpayers. In addition, Israel was a conquered and occupied territory, and the taxes were Roman taxes, the taxes of the hated enemy. For a Jew to collect those Roman taxes was to betray his own people. So Matthew was not exactly an upstanding community figure. And Jesus knew all about his reputation when He chose Him.

23

Yet Matthew, too, turned out to be a faithful disciple. He was given the privilege of writing the Gospel of Matthew, from which we learn much about the life and ministry of our Lord.

Peter was another fisherman. He was impulsive and often spoke hastily. He didn't understand God's point of view at all. He boastfully promised never to desert Christ, and later denied that he even knew Him. But again, Christ knew that He could polish this "rough gem." Peter became an important leader in the early church, was bold in his witness (he learned to use his big mouth the right way!), opened up the gospel to the Gentiles, and probably died as a martyr.

None of the men Jesus chose as His friends and followers was a saint. None was qualified for the job of changing the world. Yet Christ knew that He and the Father and the Holy Spirit could transform the lives of these men and use them to build the church.

Another surprise is *Moses*. We hear a lot about his mighty exploits for God. But he had some feelings of inferiority too. Summarize the background on Moses, taken from pages 34 and 35 of *Preparing for Adolescence.* Or, if time allows, have your students read Exodus 2:1-15; 3:1-22. Then have them read Exodus 4:1-14 and find Moses' objections and God's promises. Discuss God's attitude toward Moses' continued objections.

Have your students take a moment to think about any similarities between themselves and the Bible characters just studied, and have them jot these down on the lesson sheet. *Parent:* go through all the similarities your child suggests, and discuss them. *Teacher:* accept a few random comments.

Encourage your students to believe that God can use them if He can use people like those in the study just completed.

Compensation: share something about ways you have compensated or are compensating now, developing strengths to make up for weaknesses.

Have your students list activities they do well or like to do. Let them circle one or two they want to work on. *Parent:* help your child work out some specific steps for getting started. *Teacher:* ask your students to think of some ideas for getting started, and have a few volunteers share their thoughts.

Friends: lead a brief discussion on ways friends help one's self-concept. Encourage students to describe their friends and how the friendship helps them feel good about themselves.

Direct your students to the Scriptures and ask them to use ideas from the verses to describe the kind of friend they would like to be. Discourage copying; urge them to *adapt* and *apply* the ideas. *Examples:* "I would like to be a kinder friend to Tony, who has problems at home and doesn't need me teasing him at school." "I would like to be more forgiving, so I don't yell at my friends when they accidentally hurt my feelings."

Have your students rate themselves on the Friendship Scale. Remind them that the score they receive is not as important as the opportunity to think through ways they are doing well at being a friend, and ways they need to improve.

FINAL SUGGESTION

Parent: read the Scriptures with your child and discuss the questions given. *Teacher:* have your students work in small groups to read the Scriptures and answer questions.

Go over the closing section (the "two voices"). *Parent:* have your child roleplay both voices, and then make a decision. Or you can do the voices and let your child roleplay, making the decision. *Teacher:* have three students roleplay the voices and the decision. *Both:* if time permits, have students go beyond the "voices" given, and invent new statements for positive and negative. For example, "I'll never pass that test tomorrow." "I think I'll try making friends with Sue." "I guess there's no point in talking to Joe; he wouldn't like me anyway." "I wonder if there's some way I can help Mary."

Close with a time of quietness and prayer; encourage your students to talk to God and to commit themselves to choosing *His* voice rather than the negative voice.

Conformity: What It's All About

This lesson is based on pages 41-50 of *Preparing For Adolescence*.

"Conformity" (pronounced kun-FORM-uh-tee) means:

the need and desire to be just like everybody else...

        to do what they do
        to say what they say
        to think what they think
        to wear what they wear
        to be afraid to be different from the majority

25

Our society exerts

    to be like other people.

Young people aren't the only ones who feel they have to conform.

Why did the first woman at the orientation meeting refuse the coffee?

Why did the second woman say "No, thank you"?

Why did the other women turned down the refreshments?

We conform because . . .

We don't want to be laughed at. So we
   only do what we think is safe.

What styles are "in" right now at your school?

How do *you* feel about the idea of being "in" or "out" of style?

Are you able to be "in" style as much as you would like?

What are some other things (besides clothes) that are "in" or "out" at your school?

What happens to those who are "out"?

Have you been laughed at for not being "in"?

How did you feel?

Have you ever laughed at someone else who was out of step with the majority?

Have you **ever** thought that he or she felt as badly about being laughed at as you did?

26

Fact: The pressure to conform is at its
   worst during adolescence. That's
   why teens often herd together like a
   flock of sheep.

Remember the story of the "card game" from *Preparing for Adolescence?*

Fact: Three out of four young people studied didn't have the courage to say the group was wrong.

Have you ever been in a situation where you were sure "the group" was wrong?
What did you do?

Fact: Having just one other person agree with you helps!

Can you tell about a time when you were able to do the right thing because one other person was doing it?

Tell some of your own ideas about why young people are so afraid of being rejected by the group.

In my work with teens, I've found that the answer goes back to the issue of INFERIORITY, which I've discussed before in this Growthguide.

When you feel inferior, you are more afraid of ridicule or rejection. So you conform. You do what is "safe" so others won't put you down or laugh at you.

Here are some common fears adolescents have about rejection. Check those that bother you, and add more if I've missed some of yours.

_____ Fear that a particular group will reject you.

_____ Fear of not being invited to a party.

_____ Fear of being disliked.

_____ Fear of failure.

_____ Fear that the person you ask for a date will say no.

_____ Fear that no one will ask you for a date.

_____ _____

_____ _____

_____ _____

Tell some of the ways the young people at your school conform.

Can you guess at the fears that some of them have?

Why will the subject of conformity be important to you as you go into the adolescent years?

Can you see any reason why peer pressure could be dangerous to you?

Do you see any ways that peer pressure could get you into trouble later on?

How does conformity hurt you right now?

How does it keep you from doing what is right?

How could it interfere with your life?

28

Next time we'll talk some more about conformity and what it does to people; how to prepare to handle peer pressure; and God's view of conformity. Read the rest of Chapter 2 of *Preparing for Adolescence.*

Parent/Teacher Instructions

Begin with a discussion of conformity, based on pages 41 and 42 of *Preparing for Adolescence* and on the introductory portion of the Growthguide. Don't work on it too long, but make sure the main points get across.

Make sure your students have read the story about the job orientation and the coffee table (pages 42-45 in *Preparing for Adolescence*). If they haven't, give a summary. (*Parent:* have your child read it now.) Direct their attention to the cartoon depicting that meeting, and discuss with them the questions accompanying it.

Ask for your students' ideas on why people conform.

Discuss the series of questions about what is "in" and "out" and the feelings about being laughed at.

Make sure your students have read the story of the "card game"—or summarize it. Parent, have your child read pages 45-48 of *Preparing for Adolescence* if he or she has not already done so. Stress the point that three out of four young people studied didn't have the courage to say the group was wrong. Discuss the questions following the "card game" cartoon.

Have your students go over the list of fears, check those that bother them, and add any others they experience. Ask for some samples of the ways young people at school conform, and for suggestions on the fears that they may have.

Parent: discuss the remaining questions with your child. *Teacher:* have your students form small groups to discuss the questions. Circulate among them to get a taste of what they are saying. Summarize at the end, using ideas from *Preparing for Adolescence.*

Close with prayer, asking God to help young people resist the pressure to conform in unnecessary, dangerous, or harmful ways.

29

Lesson Five

The Pressure to Conform

This lesson is based on pages 50-61 of *Preparing for Adolescence.*

REVIEW

Last time we talked about *conformity,* and how it comes from fear of being rejected. Teens are especially apt to conform because they often have more difficulty feeling good about themselves, and so they have a greater need for the approval of their peers. In this lesson we're going to explore the subject of conformity even further, and talk about ways to deal with the pressure to conform.

If you were the person who is being urged to take the pills, what are some things you could say? What would happen if you said them?

What can conformity do to you?

It can lead you to destroy your body with . . .

> drugs
> alcohol
> cigarettes
> junk food
> and other harmful things

What can nonconformity do to you?

It might cost you some friends. (Are they *real* friends?)

BUT

It might turn you into a leader and enable you to help others make the right choices!

THINK ABOUT IT: Most teens respect a guy or gal who has the courage to be his or her own person, even when being mocked or teased.

Have you noticed some "nonconformists" at your school—people who can't be pressured into doing something wrong or harmful?

How do you feel about them?

How do others feel about them?

Have you noticed any connection between being a nonconformist and being a leader?

Have you seen examples of the way one person's courage in the face of pressure helps another person stand up for what is right?

WHAT ABOUT THOSE WHO CAN'T CONFORM?

Have you known a person with a physical handicap?

How did you and others treat that person?

How do you think that person felt?

If *you* are handicapped, share your feelings about your problem and the way it makes you feel different from others.

HOW DO YOU TREAT OTHERS?

Have you ever been teased about a physical feature you couldn't help?

How did you feel?

Have you ever teased someone else? How do you think he or she felt?

REMEMBER: You have *no business* making another person feel worse than he or she already does about some physical feature or handicap.

Sign a contract with yourself right now so that you will remember this lesson:

I, _____,
     (name)

hereby agree with myself that I will not point out, ask
questions about, or make nicknames about the
physical features or handicaps of another person. I will
remember that I have no business making another
person feel worse than he or she already does about
such problems.

Signed: _____

Date: _____

A LOOK AT THE BOOK

Read Matthew 25:31-40.

Jesus said that being kind to _____
   is the same as being kind to _____

Think of some people you know to whom you could be kind, and the ways you could be kind to each one. List them here:

People	Ways to Be Kind

Circle one name and at least one way to be kind to that person, and write in a date to indicate when you will begin.

WHAT DOES GOD THINK OF CONFORMITY?

Read Romans 12:2 in the Bible versions given here:

"Do not conform any longer to the pattern of this world, but be transformed by the renewing of your mind. Then you will be able to test and approve what God's will is— his good, pleasing, and perfect will" (*New International Version*).

"Do not conform yourselves to the standards of this world, but let God transform you inwardly by complete change of your mind. Then you will be able to know the will of God—what is good and is pleasing to him and is perfect" (*Today's English Version*).

"Don't copy the behavior and customs of this world, but be a new and different person with a fresh newness in all you do and think. Then you will learn from your own experience how His [God's] ways will really satisfy you" (*The Living Bible*).

What does this Scripture say *not* to do?

What are some examples of doing what we are not to do?

What does the Scripture say we *should* do?

What are some examples of doing what we should do?

Read Hebrews 11:24-26. Why did Moses choose not to conform?

How can knowing the Lord Jesus Christ and the promises of God help you choose **not to** conform in harmful ways?

The college student in the cartoon had a good answer in a tough situation. It's a good idea to think ahead about situations that might arise and what you will say if they do. Brainstorm some real-life predicaments that could happen to you, in which you will be pressured to conform in a way that is harmful and wrong. Then brainstorm answers you can give in each case.

Read pages 63-76 of *Preparing for Adolescence* before the next lesson.

Parent/Teacher Instructions

Briefly review the last lesson and introduce this one.

Parent: read through the first cartoon strip with your child. *Teacher:* have your students act out the cartoon strip or improvise a similar situation that they face.

Brainstorm ways to handle the situation depicted in the cartoon strip, and the consequences of various responses. (A helpful question is, "What's the worst thing that could happen if you . . . ?" This may help young people see that loss of "face" by turning down the pills isn't as bad as damaging one's body by accepting them.)

Discuss the questions up to the next heading, "What About Those Who Can't Conform?"

If your students have read the text, ask them to recall the stories about young people reflected in the artwork. If they have not read it, review the stories for them. *Teacher:* have your students form groups of three or four to discuss the questions under this heading. Circulate to get a flavor of what they are saying. Sum up and move on to the next section, "How Do You Treat Others?"

Have your students read the "Jeep Fenders" cartoon strip. Discuss the questions that follow. Point out the "contract" and give your students a minute to sign it.

Have your students read Matthew 25:31-40. Get them to give the first two answers. (Being kind *to the least of these* is the same as being kind to *Jesus*.) Then give them a few minutes to fill in the chart on being kind to people. Urge them to make a specific plan to do at least one act of kindness within the next week.

Have three different students (good readers) read the three versions of Romans 12:2. Have groups of three or four students discuss the questions about that Scripture. Circulate to get a taste of what they are saying. Sum up and move on to the Hebrews Scripture. Discuss the questions with the whole class.

Go over the cartoon of the college class. Brainstorm as suggested at the end of the lesson. Help your young people think of good ways to answer in difficult situations.

Close in prayer, thanking God that He gives the motivation and the power every Christian needs in order to resist the pressure to conform to the world.

Lesson Six

The Physical Changes of Growing Up

This lesson is based on pages 63-76 of *Preparing for Adolescence.*

In this lesson we will take a look at the physical changes that take place as you grow up. You've probably noticed that adults are not just bigger than children, but their bodies are shaped differently and work differently.

The change from a child's body to an adult's body is part of this growing-up time called adolescence. If you are ten to thirteen years of age, you will soon be experiencing some of these changes.

The "big boss" in the growing-up process is a bean-sized organ in the brain called the pituitary gland.*

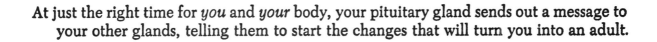

At just the right time for *you* and *your* body, your pituitary gland sends out a message to your other glands, telling them to start the changes that will turn you into an adult.

IT'S IMPORTANT FOR YOU TO KNOW WHAT'S GOING ON

Reason #1: If you don't know what is about to happen to your body, it can be terrifying when the changes start taking place.

---

*For pronunciation and definitions of terms, see the last page of this lesson.

Young people wonder . . .

Reason #2: Many young people don't know who to talk to about what is happening to them, so they suffer in silence. These lessons are planned to break that silence, to give you needed information, and to encourage you to talk to a trusted person about anything that worries you.

Have you begun to experience changes in your body?

Have you worried, not knowing why they are happening?

Have you had a hard time deciding to talk to someone about these changes?

ONE OF THE MAJOR CHANGES . . .

. . . taking place in your body is that it is beginning to *equip itself for parenthood.*

Though it should be years before you become a parent, your body needs to start getting ready now. Just as you tune a car until it's running just right, so your body has to "tune itself up" for awhile before it's ready for the big job of parenthood.

This process of getting ready is called *puberty.*

WHAT HAPPENS TO BOYS

First, let's find out what happens to boys during puberty. Then we'll talk about what happens to girls.

If you are a boy, you will find . . .

You will begin to grow faster than ever before

Your muscles will develop

You'll be stronger and better coordinated

You'll begin to grow hair . . .
—under your arms
—in your beard area
—in your pubic region
—in other areas of your body

Your sex organs will become larger

Your voice will begin to deepen

The transformation from child to adult is something like that of a caterpillar to a butterfly.

These changes can begin very suddenly, almost overnight. If you know what to expect, you won't worry so much.

What have *you* been experiencing:

____Growth?

____Developing muscles?

____Strength?

____Coordination?

____Hair?

____Sex organs enlarging?

____Voice deepening?

They're all signs that you're becoming a man!

WHAT HAPPENS TO GIRLS

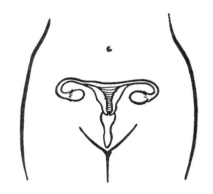

A girl's body goes through changes even more complex than those a boy's goes through, for a female body has to prepare itself for motherhood. Here's what a girl's body has to get ready to do:

Every month (approximately) a woman's body prepares the uterus with blood and other material that will be needed if the woman becomes pregnant (that is, if a baby begins to grow in her uterus).

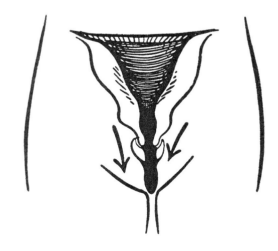

When a woman has a sexual relationship with a man, resulting in the woman becoming pregnant, the new life begins to develop in the form of a one-celled "zygote." This cell begins to divide into two, then four, then eight cells, and so on, and later becomes attached to the wall of the uterus. (Note: the zygote does not become attached.) The growing life is fed through the mother's body. It becomes large enough to be called an embryo, then a fetus, and finally is ready to be born, a complete baby.

But if pregnancy does not occur, the blood and other material that accumulated in the woman's uterus are not needed, and her body lets them flow out through the vagina. This process is called menstruation. The girl or woman who is menstruating uses a cotton pad to absorb the blood. The flow usually lasts 3-5 days.

Many girls look forward to their first menstruation; they are eager to start the process of growing up, and their first menstrual period, as it is called, is a signal to them that they are on their way.

But girls also worry, so I want to assure you—you won't bleed to death. And if you have some worries, talk to your mother, school nurse, doctor, or someone else you can trust. In 98 cases out of 100, the fears girls have are nothing to worry about once they find out the facts.

OTHER CHANGES IN GIRLS

You will probably have a growth spurt just before the time of your first menstruation. The twelfth year is usually the time of greatest growth in girls. Your body will become more rounded and curvy. Your breasts will enlarge, and may be sore at times.

You will find hair growing under your arms, on your legs, and in your pubic region.

Where are you in your growth timetable?
_____ Menstruation?
_____ Growth spurt?
_____ Curves forming?
_____ Breasts enlarging?
_____ Body hair?

PROBLEMS FOR BOYS AND GIRLS

Two problems are common to most young people going through puberty.

Problem #1: Skin trouble (pimples, acne)

Most young people get pimples and blackheads. This can be one of the most distressing aspects of all the changes that take place in puberty.

WHY do you get these blemishes?

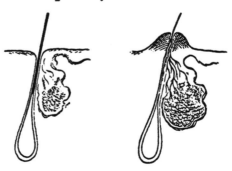

An oily substance that is secreted during adolescence tends to plug up your pores. If it can't escape, it stays there and gets hard, becoming a pimple or a blackhead.

You may have very few problems with your skin, or a lot of trouble. Your skin problems may last a short time, or they may bother you for years. Each person is different.

But you can *HELP YOURSELF* by washing your face well and often, and by eating good, healthful food and avoiding "junk food."

If your skin problems are really bad, you might ask your parents to take you to a dermatologist.

Have you had any trouble with your skin yet?

How often do you wash your face, and with what?

How are your eating habits?

Can you make up your mind to wash more and eat better, to help your skin?

Problem #2: Fatigue

Your body is using so much energy for growing up that it may not have much left over for other activities. This phase of your growth probably won't last too long, but you should be expecting it. There are two things you can do to help yourself during this time.

1. Get plenty of rest and sleep.

41

You will actually need more rest during puberty than you did when you were nine or ten. You may not want to go to bed early—"like a little kid"—but you DO NEED THE REST!

Have you been feeling tired? If so, try this:

Write down what time you go to bed (PM) and what time you get up (AM) each day:

SUNDAY	*MONDAY*	*TUESDAY*	*WEDNESDAY*	*THURSDAY*	*FRIDAY*	*SATURDAY*
PM AM	PM AM	PM AM	PM AM	PM AM	PM AM	PM AM
— —	— —	— —	— —	— —	— —	— —
hours	hours	hours	hours	hours	hours	hours

Then write in the number of hours of sleep you get each day.

How do you feel when you get up after the shortest amount of sleep you wrote down?

How do you feel when you get up after the longest amount of sleep you wrote down?

If you feel better after more sleep, can you think of some ways to get more sleep every day?

You might: sleep later in the morning
go to bed earlier at night
take a nap after school

Try getting a half-hour extra sleep every night (or day) for a week and see if you don't feel better.

And if that isn't enough, try adding *another* half hour. Don't worry about having a "little kid's bedtime"—just remember that this extra need for sleep happens BECAUSE YOU ARE GROWING UP!

2. Eat properly.

42

You probably know the basic requirements, but do you eat as well as you know you should?

Do you get enough:

Milk and dairy products?

Breads and cereals?

Fruits?

Vegetables?

Protein foods like meat, fish, poultry, nuts, cheese?

Do you skip the "junk foods," such as cupcakes, colas, candy bars, corn chips, and potato chips?

THE BRIDGE OF LATE MATURITY

Your road to adulthood not only passes the canyon of inferiority, but it also crosses the shaky bridge of late maturity.

Fact: Every person has his or her own timetable for growing up.

If your timetable is later than those of your friends, you may worry that you'll "never grow up."

But take a look at the adults around you. Do you see any who are shaped like children? No? Well, don't worry, *you too will grow up.* Just hang in there and be patient.

Special Note: Don't you be guilty of making other people your age feel badly about themselves if they grow before or after you do!

Before the next lesson, read pages 76-86 of *Preparing for Adolescence*.

GLOSSARY OF TERMS

Abdomen (AB-dō-men): The front part of your body between your waist and your legs; your "belly" or "stomach."

Acne (AK-nee): The presence of numerous pimples and blackheads.

Dermatologist (dur-muh-TOL-uh-jist): A doctor specializing in skin problems.

Embryo (EM-bree-oh): A baby in its early stages of development in its mother's uterus.

Fatigue (fuh-TEEG): Lack of energy; tiredness.

Fetus (FEE-tus): The unborn baby between the eighth week and the moment of birth.

Maturation (ma-tyoor-A-shun): The medical word for growing up.

Menstruation (men-stroo-A-shun): The process by which the body eliminates the blood and other material prepared in case a woman becomes pregnant.

Pituitary (pi-TYOO-uh-ter-ee) **Gland**: The master gland that tells the rest of your glands what to do. It starts the growing-up process in your body.

Pregnant (PREG-nunt): Carrying a developing fetus (baby) in the uterus; expecting a baby.

Puberty (PYOO-bur-tee): The period during which your body begins to equip itself for parenthood.

Pubic (PYOO-bic) **Area**: The part of your body where your sex organs are located.

Uterus (YOO-ter-us): The special place in a woman's lower abdomen where a baby grows.

Vagina (vuh-JĪ-nuh): The special opening in a woman's body which receives the man's penis, and through which the menstrual flow is released and babies are born.

Womb (WOOM): Another term for uterus.

Zygote (ZĪ-goat): The tiny cell that is the beginning of human life.

43

General Instructions: Give the factual information from this lesson as fully as time allows. Make sure you know the pronunciation and meaning of the words used. The glossary at the end of the lesson will help. Remember that your students are to read the pages from *Preparing for Adolescence,* where they will receive the same information in more complete form. Be sure to take time for the parts of the lesson that ask your students to answer questions about their self-care habits of eating, sleeping, and so on.

Parent: Take plenty of time with this lesson. Answer your child's questions as fully as you know how to. Let him or her know that you once had questions and worries about your growth. Make sure you cooperate in your child's efforts to get more sleep, eat better, and so on. For further information, assurance, or checking specific problems (pains, acne), schedule a visit with your child's physician.

Teacher: Consider the possibility of inviting a physician or other expert in adolescent growth problems to address your class. Ask her or him to speak for one-third to one-half the total class time. Then have a question-answer period. Allow ten minutes or so for your students to work individually on the parts of the lesson that ask them to examine their own habits.

Close in prayer, thanking God for the wonderful gift of the human body, and asking for guidance and help in taking proper care of it.

The Sexual You

This lesson is based on pages 76-86 of *Preparing for Adolescence.*

Along with all the growing-up changes in your body, you will begin to experience a new interest in the opposite sex. You will develop a sexual appetite. You will want to spend more and more of your time with someone of the opposite sex. Eventually this may lead you to marriage. Marriage can be wonderful when you find the right person. But please don't rush it!

45

Fact: Half of all teenage marriages blow up within five years!

Do you know anyone who got married as a teenager? How is the marriage working out?

Here are some of the feelings that your sexual development will bring:

BOYS	GIRLS
very interested in the bodies of girls . . .	fascinated with the boy himself . . .
. . . curves	. . . how he walks
. . . softness	. . . how he talks
. . . hair	. . . how he thinks
. . . eyes	
. . . feet	will get one crush after another on boys, even on older men.

WHAT ABOUT INTERCOURSE?

Sexual intercourse is a very special experience that God Himself created. It is His gift to man and woman.

Read Genesis 1:27, 28, 31 and complete the following statements:

God created _____ and _____.

He told them to be _____ and _____.

He saw what He had made, and it was _____.

God commanded the man and woman to be fruitful and multiply, and the way to do that is to have a family. The way to have children is to have sexual intercourse. So when God said that what He had made was *good,* that included sex.

However, sexual intercourse is good not only because it can produce babies, but because it gives pleasure to the man and woman. It forms a very special bond between husband and wife that no one else should share. Marriage partners have sexual intercourse regularly for no reason other than the pleasure it gives them, and to express their love for each other.

That's why God put some limits on our expression of sexual feelings. He wants us to save our sexual activity until we have the very best place for it—marriage.

Let's see what God says in His Word. Read the verses and complete the statements.

Exodus 20:14: You shall not commit _____.

(This means _____.)

First Thessalonians 4:3: It is God's will that we _____

DECIDE NOW

You will probably have an opportunity to have sexual intercourse before you are 20. And when the occasion comes, you may not have time to think through your decision. If you decide *now* what you will do *then,* your decision will be there waiting for you when you need it. Take a quiet moment and decide, then write your decision here:

I have decided that this is what I will do about sex before marriage:

_____

_____

_____

_____

SOME REASONS FOR WAITING

Venereal Disease: You can catch some very unpleasant diseases if you have sexual intercourse with a person who has these diseases. If you save yourself for marriage, and your partner does the same, you won't have to worry about these diseases.

What have you heard about venereal disease?

Do they teach you about it in school?

Have you ever thought about the danger of getting such a disease if you have sex with someone outside of marriage?

Unwanted Babies: If you have sex before marriage, you aren't prepared to raise a family. You may need to finish school, to train for a job. You may need to have some freedom to find out what you want to do with your life. If you get pregnant, or if you cause a girl to get pregnant, the rest of your life will be affected no matter what you do about the pregnancy.

What are your plans for the future?

Have you thought about what it takes to care for a baby?

How would your future plans be affected if you or your girlfriend became pregnant and you "had to" get married?

Your Mind is affected by premarital sex. You lose the innocence of youth. You can become hard and cold.

Your Future Marriage can be affected if you have sex beforehand. That relationship that should be a wonderful, special experience just for the two of you is no longer so special if others have had a sample.

Your Relationship with God, that most important of all relationships, is harmed by premarital sex. It's a sin, and you just can't be friends with God if you continue to sin deliberately.

47

Read First John 1:6. If you sin willfully and yet say you are God's friend, what does God say you are?

How important to you is your relationship with God?

Is it worth harming that relationship in order to have premarital sex?

MASTURBATION

The Bible says nothing about masturbation, so we don't really know what God thinks about it. My *opinion* is that He doesn't make a big issue of it. It *won't* cause you to become crazy, as some people say. So I would encourage you not to struggle with guilt over it.

Nocturnal Emissions

Sometimes a boy will eject some semen at night while he is sleeping. This is a natural, normal occurrence. Don't worry about it.

THE QUESTIONS OF FEAR

These are questions to talk over with a trusted adult if they are worrying you:

1. Are all these things supposed to be happening to me?

2. Is there something wrong with me?

3. Do I have a disease or abnormality?

4. Am I going to be different from other people?

5. Does this pain in my breast mean I have cancer?

6. Will I be able to have intercourse, or will there be something wrong with me?

7. Will the boys laugh at me? Will the girls reject me?

8. Will God punish me for having sexual thoughts?

9. Won't it be awful if I become a homosexual?

10. Could I get pregnant without having sexual relations?

11. Do some people fail to mature sexually?

12. Will my modesty be sacrificed?

Nearly everyone growing up in our culture worries and frets about sex. I hope this lesson will help you avoid those anxieties.

Read pages 87-104 of *Preparing for Adolescence* before the next lesson.

GLOSSARY OF TERMS

Gonorrhea (gon-uh-REE-uh): An infectious disease of the sex organs, urinary tract, rectum, and cervix, transmitted mainly by sexual intercourse.

Homosexual (hō-mō-SEK-shoo-ul): A person who has sexual desire for persons of the same sex.

Hormones (HŌR-mōnz): Substances formed by organs in your body which stimulate other parts of your body to function.

Masturbation (mas-tur-BAY-shun): Rubbing your own sex organs for sexual enjoyment.

Nocturnal Emissions (nok-TUR-nul ee-MISH-uns): The ejecting of semen at night.

Penis (PEE-nis): The male sex organ.

Premarital (pree-MAR-uh-tal): Before marriage.

Semen (SEE-mun): A whitish secretion of the male sexual organs; carries the sperm which joins to the woman's egg to form a zygote.

Sexual Intercourse (SEK-shoo-al IN-tur-kors): The act that occurs when a man's erect penis is inserted into a woman's vagina.

Syphilis (SIF-uh-lis): A chronic infectious venereal disease.

Venereal (vuh-NEAR-ee-ul) *Disease:* A disease transmitted by sexual intercourse.

Parent/Teacher Instructions

Prepare carefully for this lesson. Make sure you know how to pronounce and define the words in the glossary. As in Lesson 6, you might consider inviting an expert to address your class, allowing plenty of time for questions and for the exercises in the lesson.

Introduce the session as in the lesson sheet. Put some stress on the dangers of teenage marriages.

Parent: let your child express himself or herself as to the level of interest he or she has reached in regard to the opposite sex. (The younger ones may still be in the "yech" stage and may find it hard to believe they will *ever* develop such an interest.)

Parent: go through the Scriptures with your child in the "What About Intercourse?" section of the lesson. Talk about the "Decide Now" section. Encourage your child to share his or her decision with you, but allow your child to keep this private if he or she prefers.

Teacher: go through the Scriptures with your class in the "What About Intercourse?" section. Allow them to do the "Decide Now" section individually.

Parent: go through the rest of the lesson with your child, talking about the information provided and the questions asked. Regarding the twelve questions at the end, use *Preparing for Adolescence* and your own knowledge and experience to answer any questions that are troubling your child. If more information is needed, work with your child to research the question at the library, or ask a physician or other knowledgeable person.

Teacher: go through the venereal disease section with the whole class. Have your students form small groups to talk about "unwanted babies." Circulate to get a hint of what they are saying. Summarize your own thoughts and move on. Share information from "Your Mind" and "Your Future Marriage" sections. Have your class go through "Your Relationship with God" section together. Briefly share comments on masturbation and nocturnal emissions. If time permits, close with a question-answer period, allowing students to ask about the 12 "Questions of Fear" or any other questions related to the lesson material.

49

Above all, it is important for the leader of the group not to reveal embarrassment or anxiety when discussing the subject of sex. The moment a class (or an individual) detects tension in the leader, they will "freeze" solidly. No meaningful discussion can occur thereafter.

Close in prayer, thanking God for creating the human body and the sexual relationship, and asking Him for guidance in the proper use of His gifts.

Ah, Love!

This lesson is based on pages 87-104 of *Preparing for Adolescence*.

FOOD FOR THOUGHT:

What does it mean to fall in love?

How do you know when you're in love?

Can you be fooled?

Can you think you are in love when you aren't?

What are the characteristics of love?

What is necessary to keep a love relationship alive?

Fact: There is much confusion about . . .

What love is
>What love does
>>What love means emotionally

Fact: Most people in our society eventually want to get married. When they come into their teenage years they start thinking about that possibility.

51

Fact: The divorce rate in America is higher than in any other civilized nation in **the** world.

WHY? What happened to those wonderful feelings of love?

"BELIEFS ABOUT LOVE" QUIZ

Love is an important subject. To help you do some thinking about the meaning of love, I've prepared a brief quiz. We'll talk about five questions in this lesson, and five **more** in the next lesson. Here are the first five:

YES NO *(Check one)*

_____ _____ 1. I believe that love at first sight occurs between some people.

_____ _____ 2. I believe that it is easy to distinguish real love from infatuation.

_____ _____ 3. I believe that people who sincerely love each other will not argue and fight.

_____ _____ 4. I believe that God selects one particular person for each of us to marry, and that He will guide us together.

_____ _____ 5. I believe that if a man and woman genuinely love each other, then hardships and troubles will have little or no effect on their relationship.

Now for some answers . . .

Number 1. Love at first sight?

52

NO! You can't really love someone you don't know. You can get excited about the outer shell, but you can't love the person inside until you *know* that person.

can mislead you!

Look at the lyrics given in the chart and decide what they're saying about love. Then figure out the problems that might arise in the relationship described by the lyrics. The first one is completed as an example.

LYRICS	WHAT IT SAYS ABOUT LOVE	PROBLEMS
"Before the dance was through, I knew I was in love with you."	Love can arrive during one dance.	Love can leave during the next dance.
"I didn't know what to do, so I whispered 'I love you.'"		
"I woke up in love this day, went to sleep with you on my mind."		
"Hello, I love you, won't you tell me your name?"		
"It can't be wrong when it feels so right."		
Can you think of several more?		

Warning: Love that comes overnight can leave overnight! Don't "tie the knot" based on a feeling. Real love is more than a pleasant feeling.

Number 2. Real love or infatuation?

It is NOT easy to distinguish real love from infatuation. The emotional explosion that occurs when you are infatuated makes it hard to think clearly about *anything*. It's an exhilarating event, like a roller coaster ride.

Have you ever been infatuated? (See pages 94-98 for explanation.) What was it like?

Have you ever known someone else who was infatuated? How did he or she act?

Fact: Infatuation is very *self-centered.*

Fact: Infatuation never lasts long.

How to tell the difference between infatuation and real love:

INFATUATION	LOVE
Self-centered, thinks of I, me, mine.	Focused on the other person. You want to make him or her happy, to meet his or her needs, to satisfy his or her desires, to protect his or her interests.
Never lasts long.	Lasts even when emotions go up and down.

How can you tell the difference between love and infatuation?

Give yourself plenty of *time*. If it's real love, it will last. If it's infatuation, you'll be glad you found out.

Suggestion: Don't get married until you're in your twenties, and then only if you've gone together at least two years. Following this advice could save you a lot of heartache.

Do you know anyone who got married quickly, while infatuated? What happened when their emotions went into a downward cycle?

Do you know a married couple for whom love is genuine (as far as you can tell)? Do the man and woman always feel intense romantic feelings for each other every waking hour? Or do they have times of closeness and times of "blah" feelings, and even grumpy times?

Number 3. Love is no guarantee against disagreements.

Even people who love each other have differences of opinion . . . get tired and irritated . . . disagree and even "fight." That doesn't mean their marriage is doomed or that they made a mistake in getting married. It just means that they have to *work out* their relationship.

Think about it this way . . .

You probably have a best friend, or at least a fairly close friend, someone you really like. Think about that person when you answer these questions:

Do the two of you *always* like doing the same things?

If the two of you worked together to earn $5.00, are you sure you could agree on how to spend it?

If the two of you were given an opportunity to have an outing or trip anywhere that would allow you to go and come back in one day, would you agree at first where to go?

You can be close friends without having to agree on every little thing.

How would you work out your differences with your friend about the $5.00?

And about the trip?

Just as friends work out their differences, so do married couples.

The real problem occurs when one or both partners in a marriage has this idea in mind:

That is selfishness, and it can destroy a good marriage.

Number 4. God is not operating a matchmaking service.

What was Ralph's mistake?

Did Susan make an error too?

Have you prayed about your future spouse?

Read pages 101 through the top of 102 of *Preparing for Adolescence*. Take some time to think, then write a prayer telling God your thoughts and dreams about the marriage you would like to have.

56

Read Psalm 37:4, 5 and Proverbs 3:5, 6. What do these Scriptures have to do with choosing your marriage partner?

Number 5. Love is fragile.

Hardships and tragedies can damage a genuine love relationship.

Have you seen an example of a love relationship that was damaged by hardships or trouble? What happened?

Have you seen people who have worked successfully to keep love going in spite of problems? How did they do it?

What lessons have *you* learned about working at keeping love alive?

For next time, read the rest of Chapter 4. We'll go over the answers to the remaining five questions.

Parent/Teacher Instructions

Briefly go through the introduction. Do not ask for answers to any questions before the quiz—they are just thought-provokers.

Have your child (or students) check the "yes" or "no" column for each of the five quiz questions; encourage them to express their honest opinions in these answers.

For the answer to the first question, express your own thoughts about or experiences with "love at first sight."

Go through the chart on the lyrics of popular songs. Make sure you have read Chapter 4 in *Preparing for Adolescence* so you can point out the fallacies expressed in the lyrics and the problems that could arise in such relationships. Encourage your students to think these through on their own, of course; but it's good for you to prepare in case they need help. Urge your students to add more quotations from songs that are currently popular.

For the answer to Number 2, share your own experiences with infatuation. Your openness will help your child (or students) to be more responsive. Point out the self-centered and short-lived nature of infatuation. Tell about anyone you know who got married quickly, while infatuated. Also tell, if appropriate, how your own love relationship endures the ups and downs of emotional cycles. Perhaps you can describe a low period of your life (including all the circumstances that produced stress) when your love survived.

For Number 3, again be open (if appropriate) to talk about your own marriage, and how disagreements don't mean that it is doomed.

Help your child (or students) think through the questions about working things out with a friend. Apply the idea of "working things out" to marriage relationships. Give an example or two from your own life.

For Number 4, if desired, have your students act out the story told in the cartoon strip. Let them use their imagination to "produce" scenes depicting the marriage five or ten years later. Help them see the errors: Ralph's mistake was in thinking the dream brought a direct order from God, and he acted on it too quickly; Susan's mistake was depending on Ralph's "message from God" rather than thinking for herself and seeking guidance directly from the Lord.

Give your child (or students) time to complete the rest of this section. Have the students share prayers only if they seem willing. Call for a few volunteers to comment on the assigned Scripture.

For Number 5, tell of any cases you know (or your own experience) in which tragedy befell people, and how their marriages were affected. Share your own answers to the last question as well as listening to those of your child (or students).

Close in prayer, thanking God that He created love and marriage and knows how to preserve them.

What Is Love All About?

This lesson is based on pages 104-118 of *Preparing for Adolescence.*

We've talked about the first five questions on the "Beliefs About Love" quiz. Now let's see what you think about the remaining five questions.

"BELIEFS ABOUT LOVE" QUIZ, PART 2

YES   NO   *(Check one)*

____ ____   6. I believe that it's better to marry the wrong person than to remain single and lonely throughout life.

____ ____   7. I believe that it's not harmful or sinful to have sexual intercourse before marriage if the couple has a meaningful relationship.

____ ____   8. I believe that if a couple is genuinely in love, that condition is permanent and will last a lifetime.

____ ____   9. I believe that short courtships, six months or less, are best.

____ ____   10. I believe that teenagers are more capable of genuine love than are older people.

Now for some answers. . .

Number 6. Being single is better than having a bad marriage.

Choose your mate very carefully. Many people can testify to the loneliness and sorrow that they experience *in marriage*—a miserable marriage.

Scripture speaks of the pleasures of a good marriage, of the unhappiness of a bad marriage, and of the possibilities for service to God in the single state. Read the Scriptures listed in the chart and restate them in your own words.

GOOD MARRIAGE	BAD MARRIAGE	SINGLE LIVING
Proverbs 12:4a; 18:22; 19:14; 31:10, 28.	Proverbs 11:22; 12:4b; 25:24; 27:15.	1 Corinthians 7:8, 25-35

Number 7. Premarital intercourse *is* harmful and sinful.

Many people in our society have decided that the old rules no longer apply. They want to do as they please in sexual matters (as well as in other areas of life). But God hasn't changed. He created us and He knows what is really best for us. He gave us the Bible to show us how to live the most satisfying life possible. Look at these Scriptures and write down all that they tell you God offers (and this is just a sample!):

John 10:10b: _____

John 15:11: _____

Romans 8:37-39: _____

For what purpose does God give us rules and regulations (or laws)? Find some answers in these Scriptures:

Psalm 19:7, 8: _____

Psalm 19:11: _____

What are God's rules regarding sex?

Hebrews 13:4: _____

2 Timothy 2:22: _____

Exodus 20:14: _____

Fact: God intends your body to be for one other person—your future spouse—and NO ONE ELSE.

God gave this Commandment, not to keep you from having a good time, but because He wants you to have the best possible life and marriage, and He knows that premarital sex can harm you and your future marriage. He loves you and wants what is best for you.

Number 8. Love must be maintained.

If you don't work on it, it can die.

What are some ways people can work on their love relationships?

Number 9. Give yourself *time*.

Don't get married in a hurry. A short courtship can produce an equally short marriage—or else a long but miserably unhappy marriage.

Feelings can go up and down.

Take time to learn about your own ups and downs . . . and time to get to know the other person.

Think about the married couples you know (of all ages). Do you know how long any of them went together before getting married?

Have you heard them talk about length of courtship as related to the success of their marriage?

(Remember, there may be exceptions—people who had a short courtship and a long, happy marriage. But you're a lot safer sticking to a longer courtship so you can be sure you know what you're doing.)

Number 10. Love requires maturity.

The teenage years are a time for growing up. So much is happening to you that you may not have the capacity for the caring and giving necessary to a real love relationship. That's okay. But it can be very difficult trying to make a marriage work when you are in this growing stage. Wait until you are mature enough to give, not grab.

WHAT IS TRUE LOVE?

We've said quite a few things about love—that it is unselfish, giving, caring. Let's look at a famous Bible passage on love, First Corinthians 13. Read the whole chapter first.

Now go back through verses 4-7. As you read, write each separate description of love in the left-hand column of the chart below. Then, in the right-hand column, write down one thing you *have done*, or one thing you *could do*, which would be an example of that aspect of love.

(Since you probably aren't married, apply these characteristics of love to relationships with your friends and family.)

Two are done as an example.

1 Corinthians 13:4-7	*What I have done or could do*
Love is patient.	I didn't yell at my little brother when he played with my model airplane.
Love is kind.	I could talk to that girl at school who is always alone.

62

First Corinthians doesn't tell how love "feels"—it tells how love *acts*. Love is a commitment of your *will*. Picture a train. Your will—your determination to love—is the engine which keeps the train moving. Feelings are like the caboose—it tags along, being pulled by the train. The caboose is there, but it is not the power that makes the train run.

For the next lesson, read pages 119-132 of *Preparing for Adolescence.*

Briefly introduce the lesson; then have your child (or students) answer the five remaining quiz questions.

For question Number 6, briefly state the answer and add any supporting evidence you can give from your own experience or observations. Then get your child or students working on the Scripture study. (Students may be divided into three groups, one for each set of Scriptures. Allow each group to work, then report back to the total class.)

For Number 7, follow the procedure suggested for Number 6.

For Number 8, discuss the necessity of working on a love relationship, and ways of doing so. Encourage your child (or students) to suggest ideas, but also present some of your own successful ways of building love.

For Number 9, encourage discussion of the questions, providing insight from your own experience where appropriate.

For Number 10, briefly stress the need for maturity in love.

Scripture study: allow your child (or students) time to work on the study as instructed. Be ready to suggest ideas for the right-hand column if needed.

Go over the train illustration. Try to find an example from your own life that will show the difference between the will to love and the feelings that come with love.

Close in prayer, thanking God that He created love, and asking for His help in developing the ability to give love as a commitment of the will.

Strong Emotions of Adolescence

This lesson is based on pages 119-132 of *Preparing for Adolescence.*

Read the story of the death of my dog Pippy on pages 119-123.

Have you ever lost a pet?

What were your feelings?

Remember some "firsts" and how strong your feelings were . . .

> chocolate-covered cherry (or other special treat)
> visit to dentist
> ferris wheel or roller-coaster ride
> the most exciting thing that ever happened to you
> the most frightening
> the saddest
> the happiest

You feel everything more strongly during the adolescent years. Every experience appears "king-size."

In Chapter 5 of *Preparing for Adolescence*, I discuss six characteristics of emotions during adolescence. We'll talk about the first three now and the other three in **Lesson 11**.

1. *Emotions Are Cyclical*

Feelings go from high to low to high to low to high to low.

You may get so depressed and blue that life doesn't seem worth living.

But if you are patient and try to be positive about your situation, your circumstances and your feelings will change. Life will be great again.

But you won't stay high forever, either.

Remember: If you're at rock bottom, expect to come up. If you're emotionally high, expect to come down.

Have you experienced some of these highs and lows?

Tell about one or two highs or lows and what you think influenced them (sleep, food, health, circumstances, etc.).

Remember: The world is not the way it looks to us; our emotions distort or change the true picture.

66

2. Impressions Can Be Unreliable

Have you ever had a strong "impression"?

Tell about it. What did you do about it?

What are the suggestions made at the top of page 126 of *Preparing for Adolescence* with regard to responding to impressions?

Do you have any additional thoughts on ways to handle impressions?

HOW TO KNOW GOD'S WILL

Have you ever tried to find out God's will for you in a particular situation?

What steps did you take in your effort to learn His direction?

On pages 126 and 127 of *Preparing for Adolescence*, I give five suggestions for "How to Know God's Will." Here they are with some questions for you to discuss.

1. Talk to another person.

Do you have someone to whom you can talk about an important decision or question?

If you have never thought of this before, think through the people you know and list one or two that you might consider talking to in case of need.

2. Read the Bible for direction.

Have you ever had a question about God's will to which you found an answer in the Bible? Tell about your experience.

How would you go about finding direction from the Bible?

3. *Watch the doors that open and shut.*

Have you ever had an experience in which the direction you wanted from God was provided, at least in part, through circumstances?

4. *Give yourself plenty of time to think.*

Tell about an experience in which you weren't sure at first what to do, but a few days or weeks later you were much more confident of God's direction.

5. *Pray for God's guidance and blessing and leading.*

When you're trying to decide what to do, do you remember to talk to God about it?

Tell about a time when He answered your prayers for guidance.

3. *Declaration of Independence*

When in the course of human events it becomes necessary for one adolescent to dissolve the parental bands...

Prediction: You and your parents will experience some irritation, tension, and harsh feelings about one another in the next few years.

How can I predict that?

Because I know that some stressful changes will soon occur in your relationship.

Read pages 127 and 128 of *Preparing for Adolescence*, starting with "The Declaration of Independence" and stopping at the heading "Completely Free."

List some privileges and responsibilities that you have now, but did not have five years ago.

I AM FREE TO . . .	*I AM RESPONSIBLE TO . . .*

Read pages 128-131 of *Preparing for Adolescence*, from "Completely Free" to "My Message."

What are some freedoms that you are asking for that your parents do not want to give you yet?

What are some responsibilities your parents want you to assume that you are not willing to take on?

Would you like to negotiate with your parents to see if they will grant you one freedom in exchange for a new responsibility? Talk it over and see what happens.

Read "My Message" on pages 131-132 of *Preparing for Adolescence*. If you were to receive this message from your parents, how would you respond? Write your answer here.

Read pages 132-139 of *Preparing for Adolescence* before the next lesson.

Parent/Teacher Instructions

If your students have not already read the assigned pages, have them read pages 119-122 now. If they *have* done the reading, ask them to tell you the story of the death of Pippy. Discuss the related questions.

"Emotions are cyclical"—ask if your child has ever experienced extreme ups and downs. Point out that neither the highs nor the lows last forever. Explore the elements that may have influenced the feelings (sleep, health, food, circumstances, etc.).

"Impressions"—discuss the various questions in this section, sharing experiences of your own that may be helpful.

Go through the section on God's will, again sharing anything from your own life that may be pertinent.

"Declaration of Independence"—help your students think through their new freedoms and responsibilities.

For the question on negotiation, if you are a parent studying with your child, you might try to work out at least one "trade" or compromise right now. If you are a teacher, encourage your students to talk with their parents and to show a willingness to assume new responsibilities.

For the response to "My Message" in a class, have your students write their answers. If you are a parent, allow your child either to write or to speak directly to you, whichever he or she chooses.

Close in prayer.

Lesson Eleven

More on Emotions

This lesson is based on pages 132-139 of *Preparing for Adolescence.*

In our last lesson we discussed three aspects of the emotions of adolescence—their cyclical nature, the unreliability of impressions, and the teenager's declaration of independence. Now we'll look at three more characteristics of that age.

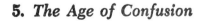

4. *No Longer Mommie's Baby*

The desire for independence creates a sensitivity among adolescents about being seen with mom and dad. You want your friends to think you are grown up, and being seen with your parents seems babyish.

Have you begun to experience this sensitivity?

Under what circumstances do you most wish *not* to be seen with your parents?

Are there places or times when it's okay to be seen with your parents?

How do your parents feel about the situation?

Remember—this doesn't mean you don't love your parents. It's just another "trial" of the teenage years. You'll get over it.

5. *The Age of Confusion*

Fact: It is common and natural for the adolescent to examine and question each of the beliefs he or she has been taught.

HEY! WAIT A MINUTE! DO I REALLY BELIEVE WHAT I'VE BEEN TOLD? HOW DO I KNOW MY PARENTS ARE RIGHT?

It can be confusing and distressing, but this time of questioning is important to your growth. It's a time for you to develop your *own* values and your own relationship with God. And more often than not, you'll find that you agree with your parents anyway.

Have you begun to ask questions and search for your own answers?

Here are some questions many teens ask. Circle those that you are wondering about, and add any I've missed.

Is there really a God?

Does He know me?

Does He care about me?

Do I believe in the values my parents have taught?

Do I want what they want for my life?

Does my experience say different things from what I have been taught?

_____

_____

_____

How do you plan to find answers to your questions?

6. *The Search for Identity*

Another major event of adolescence is finding out who you are.

Here are some questions to help you see how you are doing in your own search for identity.

Do you know who you are?

Do you know what you want in life?

Do you know your strengths and weaknesses?

Do you know what you believe about God?

Do you like the "image" your friends have of you?

Do you know what's important to you?

Do you know what's not important to you?

72

How to "find yourself"—

Try a variety of experiences . . .

    go out for various sports

    learn to play a musical instrument

    . . . to sew

    . . . to cook

    . . . to perform car-maintenance chores

    . . . to make household repairs

Ask the counselors at school to give you interest tests and vocational inventories.

Underline any of the ideas listed above that you are already doing or have done. Circle any that you would like to try. Write down how and when you are going to try them:

YOUR IDENTITY AS MALE OR FEMALE

What are your ideas right now of what makes a person a man or a woman?

MAN	WOMAN

Where did you get those ideas?

Is there a person of your own sex that you could watch and identify with to learn more about being a man or a woman?

Write his or her name on the following page and then list as many characteristics as you can that seem to be what makes him or her special as a man or woman. Later, as you watch the person more and more, you can add to your list.

NAME: _____

CHARACTERISTICS: _____

_____

_____

_____

_____

_____

_____

_____

I hope you will use this course as a springboard to learn more about yourself. You might discover that you are a really nice person!

For next time, read pages 141-163 in *Preparing for Adolescence.*

Parent/Teacher Instructions

Briefly review the last lesson.

Begin this lesson with discussion of Number 4—"No Longer Mommie's Baby." (Note: if you are a parent, and your child has already begun to shun you in public, your own emotions may be aroused in this discussion. Try to understand that this behavior does not reflect a lack of filial love, but rather is a "trial" for the teenager as well as for yourself. If you weather this storm with continued love and acceptance—and a dash of good humor—your future relationships with your child will be enhanced.)

For Number 5, encourage your child (or students) to openly discuss questions and searchings. Again, parent, this may seem threatening to you. Nevertheless, it is an inevitable process for most teenagers. It is reassuring to know that most young people eventually accept many of their parents' values and beliefs. We are promised in the Scriptures, "Train up a child in the way he should go, and *when he is old* he will not depart from it" (Proverbs 22:6).

For Number 6, in a class, have your students form small groups to discuss the questions about identity. Reassemble for whole-class discussion of "how to find yourself." The students may learn from one another, and may receive new encouragement to try something unfamiliar.

Take the class through the "Man-Woman" chart. Let your students identify their role model and that person's characteristics individually. However, if time allows and your students are open, have a few share their answers.

Close in prayer, thanking God for His love and understanding, and seeking His help in the matters discussed in this lesson.

Rap Session, Part One

This lesson is based on the first part of the "rap session" recorded in Chapter 6 of *Preparing for Adolescence*. Read pages 141-163 (stop at the "break").

Woody Allen wrote that his only regret in life was that he wasn't somebody else. Who would you like to be if you could be somebody else? Why?

When I asked about feelings of inferiority, my four friends told me their stories:

Gaylene: "My father died when I was going through physical and emotional changes. I entered junior high school without knowing who I was. I wasn't involved in anything and I had nothing to look forward to."

Darrell: "I was different from my friends because I enjoyed schoolwork. I didn't get involved in the junior high activities at church, except for a beach trip, where I was teased throughout the day."

Ceslie: "At the beginning of my first year in junior high I knew only a few people. I was short—only 4'-9" The meanest girl in the school, who was 5'-8" and was called 'Big Bertha,' kicked me for no reason."

Page: "I broke a leg and had to wear crazy-looking elevated shoes. But I used to sneak my regular shoes out of the house to wear at school so people wouldn't laugh at me."

Of these four young people, with whom do you identify most closely? Who has a problem or expresses feelings most like yours? _____

Look through pages 141-163 quickly, reading the comments of the person you just selected. Find answers to the two questions on the following page.

1. What did parents or other adults suggest to this person to help with the problem?

2. What did the person learn or figure out on his or her own as a solution to the problem?

Are you able to talk to your parents about your experiences, your questions, your fears, your triumphs?

Have you ever found yourself echoing your parents' advice when you talk to a younger brother or sister, as Darrell and Gaylene did?

Describe the various "groups" in your school and what each group expects of its members (what you have to do, or what you have to be like, to be "in" with that group).

Which of the groups do you think would be most helpful to you if you want to be God's person?

What are the difficulties you might face if you chose to identify with the group you just named?

Here is a list of some of the problems mentioned in the first half of the rap session. Pick one that troubles you particularly and discuss why you are bothered by it. Try to figure out one or two specific steps you can take to deal with or solve the problem. (If the situation is one you can't change, such as a physical flaw or disability, try to identify methods of changing the way you think about the problem or about yourself, or the way you relate to other people because of the problem.)

Not knowing who you are

Being rejected by friends because you like schoolwork

Being teased because of your clothing

Being too short

Being too tall

Having a physical disability

Feeling pressure to take drugs

Feeling pressure not to show your feelings (to be "cool")

Having freckles

Having acne

My problem: _____

Why it bothers me: _____

_____

_____

What I plan to do: _____

77

_____

_____

_____

_____

The first half of the rap session concluded with some thoughts about the acceptance offered by Jesus Christ. Look up the following Scriptures and write a brief summary of each one, showing what it tells you about God's acceptance of you and His love for you.

Romans 5:6-8: _____

_____

_____

Romans 6:23: _____

_____

_____

Ephesians 2:4-9:_____

_____

_____

1 John 4:9, 10:_____

_____

_____

For next time, read pages 163-182 in *Preparing for Adolescence.*

Parent/Teacher Instructions

This lesson is based on the first half of the "rap session" recorded in Chapter 6 of *Preparing for Adolescence.* You may conduct the lesson by using the study guide and the suggestions given here. However, you might want to consider an alternative. For a class, you could invite several teens who are three to five years older than your students. Let them form a panel to discuss the questions found in the rap session and this study guide. Encourage your students to ask as many questions as they like. For a parent, ask an older brother or sister or friend (preferably the same sex as the child who has been studying this course) to meet with you and discuss the questions found in the rap session and the study guide.

If you prefer to conduct the session in the usual way, here are some suggestions.

Briefly discuss with your students who they would like to be if they could be someone else. Then have them review the comments of the four teens and tell the one with whom they identify most closely. (If a student says none of them come close, ask him to pick one to work with anyway.) Give them some time to skim through the assigned pages and find the answers to the two questions about their selected personality.

Lead the class in discussing the questions about talking to parents and about groups in school.

Have your students work individually to select a problem and find one or two specific steps to deal with it. Move around the room, helping students think of specific actions or new ways of relating to problems.

Introduce the Bible study section. Allow students to form groups of three or four to work on this section. Reassemble and call for a few reports. Stress God's love of us *"while we were yet sinners."* He loved us while we were His enemies, and He took *action* which enabled us to come to Him and be His children. He did it all, because He loves us.

Close in prayer.

Rap Session, Part Two

In this session we will continue with our discussion of the rap session recorded in Chapter 6 of *Preparing for Adolescence* (pages 163-182).

DRUGS

The teens at the rap session talked about drugs quite a bit.

Is there a problem with drugs at your school?

Do any of the people you know use drugs?

Have you ever been offered drugs?

How have you dealt with the pressure to take drugs?

Brainstorm some good answers to use when someone offers you drugs. (You probably did this in an earlier lesson, so try to think of some new ideas. Have you tried out any of the earlier answers? What happened?)

On page 166-167 Greg says that if your friends are getting into drugs and offering them to you, you should look for some new friends. How do you feel about this statement?

Should a Christian young person try to be friends with people who use drugs, and try to win these people to the Lord? Or is it too dangerous, because the Christian might get pressured into using drugs too? What do you think, and what have you and your friends experienced?

Another topic the rap session covered was . . .

PHYSICAL CHANGES

Gaylene (pages 169 and following) was frightened when physical changes began happening to her. They started so early that her mother hadn't told her about them yet.

Darrell, Gaylene, Ceslie, and Page all experienced embarrassment about changing clothes and taking showers in their junior high school physical education classes.

Page talked about feeling inferior because his muscles weren't as strong as those of some of the other boys.

Have you been frightened or embarrassed about the physical side of adolescence?

Has the information in this course helped you to get over some of the fear or worry?

John Styll said (page 174), "God made everybody the way they are for a reason, and He doesn't make mistakes. I've met a few people who understood that principle and refused to let their imperfections bother them."

Do you agree or disagree? Why?

What do you think is the best way for a person to deal with his or her imperfections?

What are some of your imperfections, and how are you dealing with them?

On page 177 we began to discuss the idea of shopping around for your hidden abilities and talents—trying different things until you find an activity or skill you really like. This was suggested earlier in this course. Have you tried anything new yet? How did it work out?

If you haven't tried a new activity, have you thought about it?

Is there something you would like to do?

What would help you get into it?

FINAL MESSAGE

The "Final Message" is found on pages 183-185. In it I have three important thoughts for you.

First: Today is not forever

The problems that are troubling you now will go away. Things will change. Tomorrow will be different.

Second: Normality will return

Adolescence is a tough time—but you will grow through it and out of it. You will become an adult, and the difficulties of the teenage years will just be a memory.

Third and most important: Remain friends with Jesus Christ

He knows what you're going through. He understands . . . and He loves you.

Take some time right now to tell what Jesus means to you.

81

In this lesson, as in Lesson 12, you have some options. You may choose to conduct the lesson in the normal way. However, if there is a drug problem of some severity in your community, you might want to invite to your class someone who can provide drug-abuse education. (Contact your pastor, member of the local police force, representative of the local hospital, or schools for suggestions.) If it is possible to get a speaker who is a Christian, this will be ideal. If not, be sure to allow time to have your students think through, from a Christian point of view, the implications of drug abuse.

As a parent, you may want to take your youngster to visit the local police, hospital, or other facility that has drug-education materials.

If you don't feel the need to focus on drug abuse, you may want to invite as guest speaker a physician or other specialist in the area of adolescent physical changes. This was suggested earlier in this course; if you were unable to do it at the time, or if you feel that another session will be helpful, this is your opportunity.

If you choose to conduct the session in the usual way, here are some suggestions.

Go through the questions about drugs. The lesson suggests brainstorming answers to use when offered drugs. If you did this when suggested in an earlier lesson, ask your students if they have any new ideas, or if they have had opportunities to use the earlier answers.

Discuss the questions about involvement with people who use drugs.

Go through the section on physical changes. Then call for discussion of the remarks by John Styll. Lead a general discussion of the questions about exploring new activities.

Summarize the final three remarks ("The Final Message"). Give your students time to write out what Jesus means to them. (Parent: allow your child to tell you verbally if he or she prefers.)

Close in prayer.

82

Study Notes

86